Big Machines Float!

Catherine Veitch

Heinemann
LIBRARY
Chicago, Illinois

Edited by Helen Cox Cannons and Kathryn Clay
Designed by Tim Bond and Peggie Carley
Picture research by Mica Brancic and Tracy Cummins
Production by Helen McCreath
Originated by Capstone Global Library Ltd
Printed and bound in China by Leo Paper Group

18 17 16 15 14
10 9 8 7 6 5 4 3 2 1

Cataloging-in-publication information is on file
with the Library of Congress.
ISBN 978-1-4846-0587-5 (Hardcover)
ISBN 978-1-4846-0594-3 (eBook PDF)

Photo Credits
Alamy: © epa european pressphoto agency b.v., 10, 11, © Ken Gillespie
Photography, 4, 5; Corbis: © Yogi, Inc, 18, 19; Getty Images: DON EMMERT/AFP,
21, Dorling Kindersley/Richard Leeney, 22a, 8, 9, E+/Dane Wirtzfeld, 14, 15, 22c,
Joe Raedle, 17 inset, McClatchy-Tribune/Miami Herald, 16, 17; Planet Solar: ©
2013 Anthony Collins, 13 inset, © 2013 Philip Plisson, 12, 13, 22d; Shutterstock:
Nightman1965, 22b, 6, 7, back cover, Steve Woods, front cover; Wikimedia
Commons: United States Navy, LTJG Chuck Bell, 20, back cover

Every effort has been made to contact copyright holders of material reproduced
in this book. Any omissions will be rectified in subsequent printings if notice is
given to the publisher.

All the Internet addresses (URLs) given in this book were valid at the time of go-
ing to press. However, due to the dynamic nature of the Internet, some
addresses may have changed, or sites may have changed or ceased to exist
since publication. While the author and publisher regret any inconvenience this
may cause readers, no responsibility for any such changes can be accepted by
either the author or the publisher.

Contents

Some words are shown in bold, **like this.** You can find out
what they mean by looking in the glossary.

Break It Up

Ice breakers use a giant **scoop** to break up ice on a frozen river.

Ice breakers are used for **polar** research and to bring supplies to **arctic** areas.

Floating Crane

Cranes use large **booms** to lift heavy objects into the air. A floating crane can lift sunken ships off the bottom of the sea.

Super

Big

Mighty

Size

The world's largest floating crane is the Thialf. It can lift more than 11,000 tons (10,000 metric tons)!

Huge Hovercraft

A hovercraft sits on a huge cushion filled with air. It can travel over land, ice, and water.

Super
Big Mighty
Size

The world's largest hovercraft can carry up to 418 passengers and 60 cars.

Coast Garde
Guard côtière

AIRCRAFT LIFERAFTS

Fisheries Pêches
and Oceans et Océans

CH-CGD

Wide Load

This **vessel** is called a **cargo** ship. It carries cargo in containers as large as houses. A single cargo ship can carry 16,000 containers.

Cargo ships are as big as four football fields or five giant Airbus planes.

Super

Big

Mighty

Size

container

Fun in the Sun

Planet Solar's **solar-powered** boat gets its power from the sun. Solar panels help charge the boat's battery.

TURANOR PlanetSolar

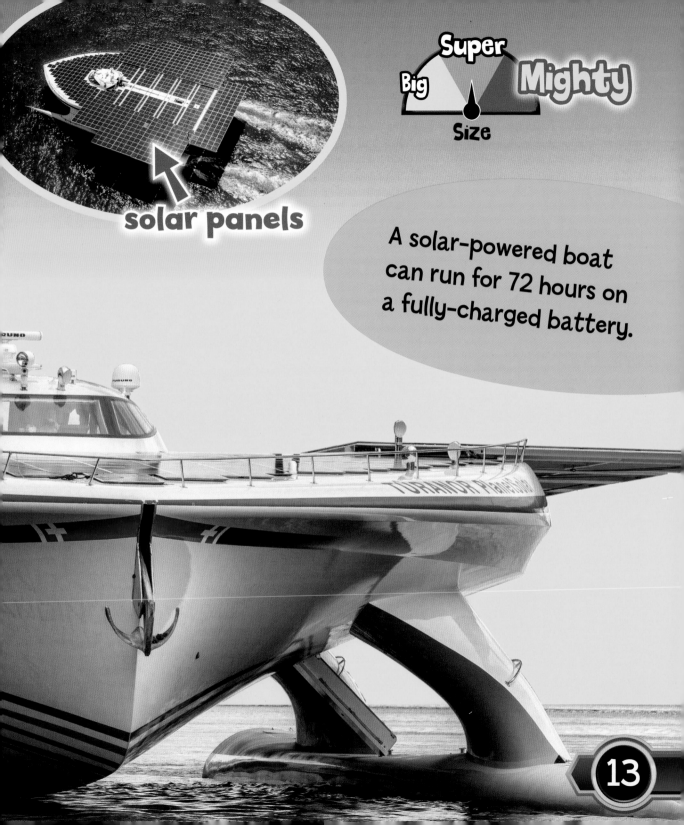

solar panels

Super

Big

Mighty

Size

A solar-powered boat can run for 72 hours on a fully-charged battery.

Mast From the Past

More than 300 years ago, people sailed in huge ships called **galleons.**

sail

mast

Galleons use wind power to move. Huge sails attach to tall **masts**. Sails catch the wind and push boats forward.

Cruise Ship

People take vacations on cruise ships. This ship can carry up to 5,400 passengers!

People can shop, ice skate, and even surf on cruise ships!

Super Sub

Submarines are light enough to float. But they spend most of their time underwater. Some subs stay underwater up to six months.

The world's largest submarine is the *Typhoon*. It is 515 feet (157 meters) long and 70 feet (21 meters) wide.

Big
Super
Mighty
Size

Sizing Things Up

Blue Marlin

Capacity	up to 60 passengers
Length	738 feet (225 meters)
Cruise Speed	17 miles (27 kilometers) per hour
Special Feature	can carry an oil rig

BLUE MARLIN

Freedom of the Seas

Capacity	up to 3,634 passengers and 1,300 crew members
Length	1,112 feet (339 meters)
Cruise Speed	25 miles (40 kilometers) per hour
Special Feature	has a full-sized basketball court

Quiz

How much of a Machine Mega-Brain are you?
Can you match each machine name to its correct photo?

floating crane • **hovercraft**
solar-powered boat • **galleon**

1

2

3

4

Check the answers on the opposite page
to see if you got all four correct.

Glossary

arctic extremely cold and wintry

boom a mechanical arm

cargo things carried by a ship

galleon a large sailing ship used 300 to 400 years ago

mast a tall pole on a boat's deck that holds its sails

polar having to do with the icy regions around the North or South Pole

scoop a hollow part for lifting things

solar-powered electricity made using the sun's light and heat

vessel a large boat or ship

Find Out More

Books

Ipcizade, Catherine. *Big Boats*. Big. Mankato, Minn:
    Capstone Press, 2010.

Swanson, Jennifer. *How Submarines Work*. Mankato,
    Minn.: Child's World, 2012.

Websites

www.discoverboating.com/kids.aspx
www.kidsdiscover.com/shop/issues/boats-for-kids/

Index